AF646595

Collins

FOUNDATION LEVEL 1

LITTLE LEARNERS

GENERAL AWARENESS

SERIES EDITOR: RANI T.

Published by Collins Learning
A division of HarperCollins*Publishers*
India Private Limited

HarperCollins Publishers
Building No 10, Tower A, 4th Floor,
DLF Cyber City, Phase II, Gurgaon 122002

1 London Bridge Street, London, SE1 9GF,
United Kingdom

2 Bloor Street East, Toronto, Ontario M4W
1A8, Canada

Lvl 13, 201 Elizabeth Street (PO Box A565,
NSW, 1235), Sydney NSW 2000, Australia

195 Broadway, New York, NY 10007, USA

Browse the complete Collins catalogue at
www.collins.in
For any queries/feedback, please write to us
at **SCHOOLSUPPORT@harpercollins.co.in** or
call us on 0124-4894800.

First published in 2020
© HarperCollinsPublishers India Private
Limited 2020

Reprint: 10 9 8 7 6 5 4 3 2 1

ISBN: 978-935357-036-1

Collins ® is a registered trademark of
HarperCollins*Publishers* Limited

All rights reserved. No part of this book may be reproduced, stored in retrieval system, or transmitted in any form or by any means, electronic, mechanical, photocopying, recording or otherwise, without the prior permission in writing of the Publisher. This book is sold subject to the conditions that it shall not, by way of trade or otherwise, be lent, re-sold, hired out or otherwise circulated without the publisher's prior consent in any form of binding or cover other than that in which it is published and without a similar condition including this condition being imposed on the subsequent purchaser.

Artwork and layout by
Qualibre Creatives Pvt. Ltd.

Printed and bound by
MicroPrints India, New Delhi

Acknowledgements

Cover: HarperCollins*Publishers*India

Title Page: HarperCollins*Publishers*India

Prelim Pages: radenmas, denkcreative, nonohana, graphic-bee

Inside: pg 8: pijama61, **pg 9:** pijama61, eliflamra, pijama61, VectorMoon,exxorian; **pg11:** Shendart, eliflamra,Tomacco,sonicken, **pg 13:** eliflamra, pijama61,eliflamra; **pg 14:** graphic-bee, eliflamra,pijama61,Julia Lemba,15RamCreativ,Denis Maliugin,eliflamra; **pg 16:** kbeis,Sudowoodo; **pg 17:** pijama61; **pg 18:** calvindexter; **pg 19:** MicrovOne, **pg 20:** stevegraham,pijama61,Morrison1977,Yosuke Hasegawa,Tetiana Lazunova; **pg 21:** stevegraham, Morrison1977,Yosuke Hasegawa; pg 23: luplupme; **pg 24:** Tigatelu,Chereliss,KanKhem; **pg 25:** rebenok, Tigrezzi,graphic-bee,colematt,Yulia Melnyk,pijama61; **pg 27:** pijama61,NiwatSingsamarn, MatoomMi; **pg 28:** Irina_Qiwi,graphic-bee, pijama61, nyamol, Guzaliia Filimonova; **pg 29:** bubble86; **pg 31:** elenabs, Xana_KR, Naddiya,lukpedclub,MaksimYremenko,Pacharada17, Ashrafali Aezazi; **pg 35:** AlexBannykh; **pg 36:** kathykonkle, StudioBarcelona,Hein Nouwens, MaksimYremenko, good_ reason08,SiberianPhotographer,Naddiya,Thirawatana Phaisalratana; **pg 37:** Nayanba Jadeja,Pathlord; **pg 38:** Sudowoodo,yayayoyo, MaksimYremenko,Denis08131,EgudinKa mayramagalhaes; **pg 39:** Aratehortua; **pg 41:** Nana555, iNueng, lukpedclub, sldesign78,Syuzanna Guseynova,"sanlas"; **pg 43:** ourlifelooklikeballoon, rosinka; **pg 44:** krishnapriya,Denis08131,VectorPocket, JuliarStudio,INDECcraft, stockillustration, Svetlana, Malysheva, FancyTapis,aqabiz,divyesh kachhdiya,Pavel Naumov,Iuliia Kanivets; **pg 47:** MarkRyanDesigns,pijama61,nyamol,VectorMoon eliflamra,pijama61; **pg 48,49:** Khabarushka, blueringmedia,RaStudio,Mykyta Dolmatov,KanKhem; **pg 50:** pijama61,lumpynoodles,graphic-bee,Sudowoodo,tanda_V, AKARAKINGDOMS, andegro4ka,Hein Nouwens,eliflamra; **pg 51:** Photoplotnikov,MaksimYremenko, IrynaDanyliuk,StudioBarcelona,Aleksander Zhelonkin,PixeLae,Yevhenii Dubinko,Vijay Patel,undefined undefined; **pg 52:** exxorian, sabelskaya,KanKhem, IconicBestiary,IconicBestiary; **pg 54:** ojogabonitoo,Jennifer Borton,siiixth,Vectoraart; **pg 55:** 9comeback; pg 58: VladSt,Usagi-D,DivVector; **pg 59:** Yutthaphan,eestingnef,eliflamra,IconicBestiary

Preface

Collins Little Learners, comprising 20 books in all, provides graded, age-appropriate learning opportunities targeting holistic skill development for children in the age group of 3 years to 6 years. Spread across three levels, the series spans **English**, **Maths**, **General Awareness**, **Art and Craft** and **Hindi**. The series comes bundled with a **workbook** for English and a book of **rhymes and stories** for each level. The books use a combination of hands-on activities, frequent recapitulation and child-friendly artwork to facilitate learning.

The early years are the most significant years for growth, development and learning. During this period, children need adequate opportunities for stimulating experiences as these favourably affect various learning abilities. Learning experiences, when chosen and planned properly, fuel the innate curiosity of children, and stimulate their thought processes.

Learning and Development During the Early Years

The goal of learning during the early years is to enhance the all-round development of personality and to inculcate healthy attitudes, life skills and good values. Creative play, well thought-out games and developmentally appropriate activities help children develop the necessary skills to achieve these goals. The skills that children need to acquire can broadly be categorized as:

Motor: Motor skills pertain not only to gross motor activities like walking and jumping but also include fine motor activities like the ability to hold a pencil and write. The development of motor skills is facilitated through several graded activities.

Personal, Social and Emotional: Personal, social and emotional development, necessary for the overall personality development of children, is achieved using a combination of hands-on activities, role plays and thought-provoking stories and rhymes.

Linguistic: The ability to listen, speak, read and write is critical to success in formal learning environments.

Mathematical: The development of mathematical ideas and concepts is important at this stage since children will continue to build on this learning for most of their years of schooling.

Knowledge and Understanding of the World: This is achieved through activities that enable children to explore their surroundings at home and in the school, and interact with the people that they see around them.

Health and Safety: The idea of health and safety is introduced through activities, stories and retelling of real-life experiences to encourage children to focus on health and well-being.

Creative: Creative skills are developed through a host of activities involving art, craft, painting, roleplays, etc.

Logical and Rational Thinking: Activities that involve simple puzzles, pattern-completion and visual discrimination help children to develop logical and rational thinking skills.

The Collins Little Learners Teacher Support Materials

The series includes extensive teacher support in the form of:

Teacher's Resource Books: Comprises stories, activity banks, classroom management and assessment guidelines

Multimedia eBook: Consists of animations, audio, video, slide shows and interactive exercises

Print-ready Worksheets: Additional worksheets for practice and reinforcement, present in the digital support

Digital Flashcards: Flashcards with embedded sounds and animations for letter formation and letter-sound association

Animations and Songs: Animated stories and rhymes set to tune

Interactive Games: Interactivities to reinforce concepts in a fun and engaging manner

A note on the activity banks (included in the Teacher's Manuals)

The activity banks comprise hands-on activities that will help children develop the requisite skills to attain age-appropriate learning goals. In keeping with Howard Gardener's theory of multiple intelligences, the activity banks include options and variations that enable teachers to provide a planned cycle of experiences and opportunities, which foster each type of intelligence, to every child in their classrooms. The activity banks equip teachers to use the strengths of children as a means of complementing their less developed areas by valuing and nurturing the inherent abilities of the children.

Contents

Walkthrough

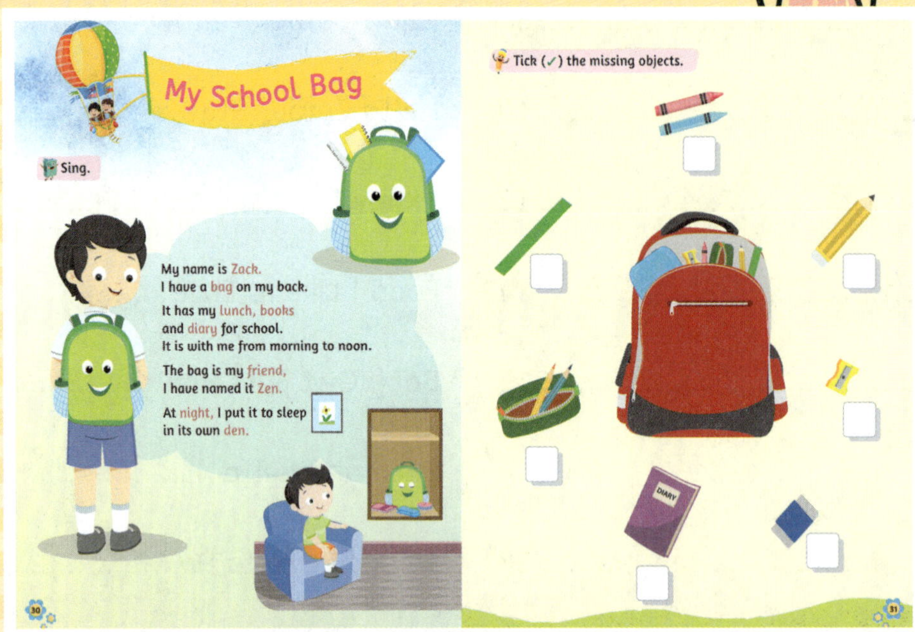

Short rhymes, set to tune, used to introduce fact-based concepts to facilitate recall. Follow-up practice exercises help reinforce the concept learnt.

Varied revision activity formats to ensure holistic skill development.

Stories used to introduce ideas of safety, helping, sharing, eating healthy, etc.

Two-page spreads used to depict real-world situations. The use of complete sceneries enables teachers to go beyond the immediate concept and engage students in activities, discussions, etc. to develop good habits, civic sense, etc.

I Am Special!

Paste your picture.

Tick (✓) the correct option.

I am a

☐ girl

☐ boy

Print your left palm.

Tick (✓) the things you like to do.

Cara's Toys

Look at these pictures. Talk about them.

Listen to the story of Cara.

Help Cara and Sana reach their toys.

Help Ron get his skateboard.

My Body Parts

Touch the picture. Name what you see.

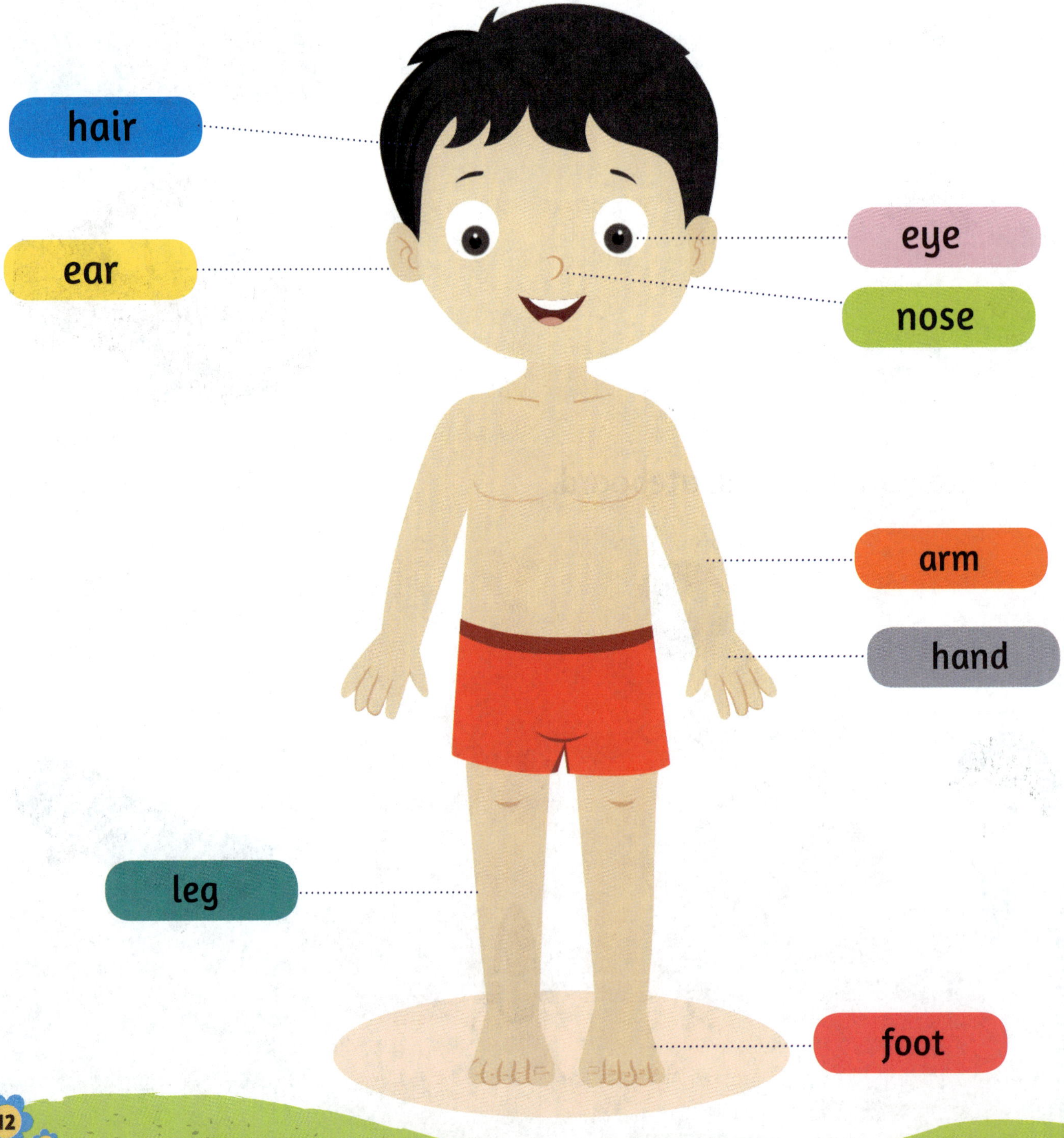

Tick (✓) the correct image.

Keeping Clean

Tick (✓) the things that you do to keep clean.

I wash my hands before eating.

☐

I wash my hands after eating.

☐

I bathe daily.

☐

I brush my teeth daily.

☐

I throw waste in a dustbin

☐

Pita and Bita

Listen to the story of Pita and Bita.

I Know!

Match the picture to the word.

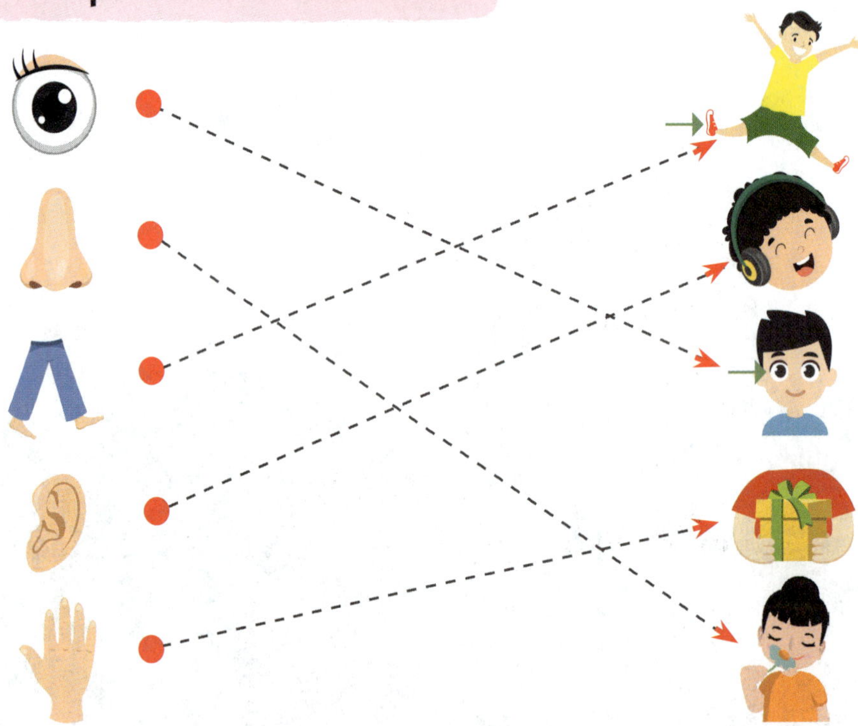

legs

ear

eye

hand

nose

Trace the patterns on the toy. Colour the toy.

Tick (✓) the correct image.

My Family

Paste your family picture.

Touch the pictures. Name what you see.

My Home

Touch the pictures. Talk about them.

Paste the correct stickers.

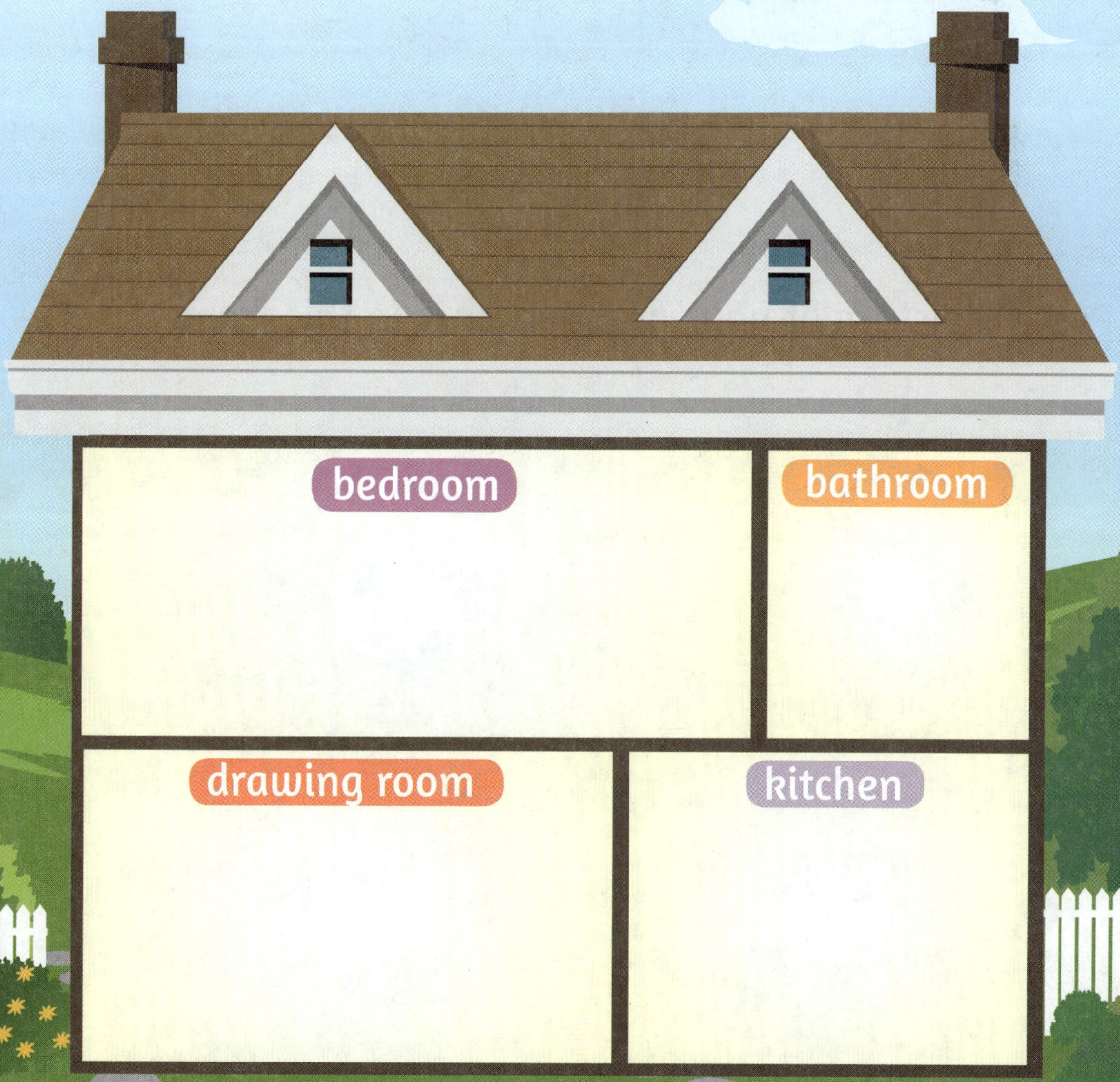

I Know!

Count and write the number of members in your family.

I have .... members in my family.

Paste a picture of your grandparents in this frame.

Place ice-cream sticks to make a house.

Day and Night

Look at the pictures. Talk about them.

Paste the correct stickers.

Greetings

Look at the pictures. Talk about each picture.

Trace the patterns.

Good Night!

Good Morning!

Thank You!

Welcome!

My School

Touch the pictures. Talk about what you see.

I read.

I have fun.

I learn.

I play.

Trace and colour to complete the image.

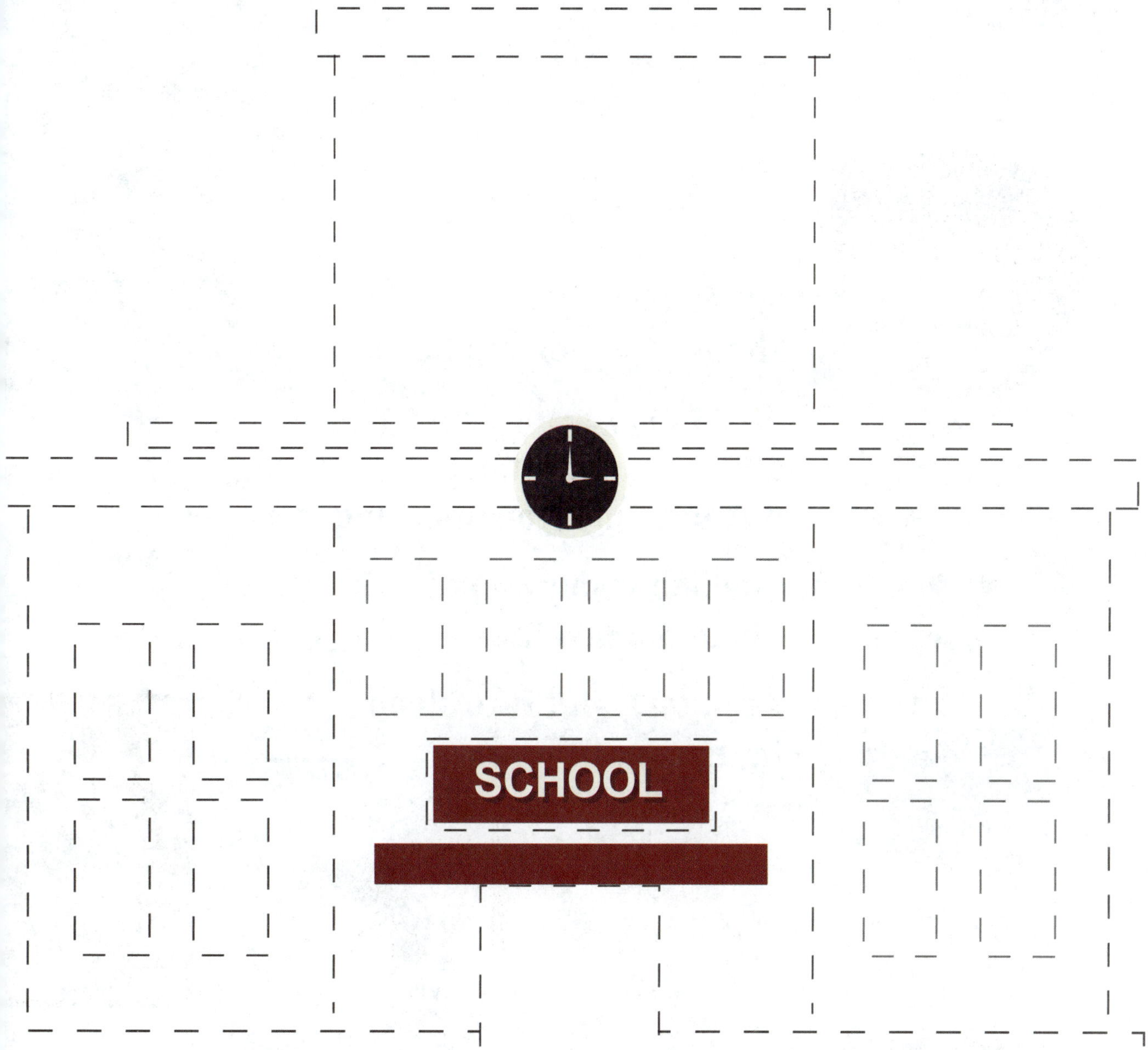

My School Bag

Sing.

My name is Zack.
I have a bag on my back.

It has my lunch, books
and diary for school.
It is with me from morning to noon.

The bag is my friend,
I have named it Zen.

At night, I put it to sleep
in its own den.

Tick (✓) the missing objects.

Manners

Sing.

We don't shout,
We don't eat with our open mouth.
When we sneeze, we cover our mouth
And say, 'Excuse me please!'
Good manners are easy,
Let's learn to say thank you,
please and sorry!

Look at these pictures. Talk about them.

Say Excuse me!

Cover your mouth and sneeze!

Don't shout!

Say Please and Thank you!

Don't run on the road!

Fun Time

Spot 3 differences between the pictures.

Join the dots to complete the picture. Colour it.

Hello Colour Red

Touch the pictures. Name what you see.

red crayon

lady bird

tomato

danger

apple

rose

pomegranate

Tear and paste red paper.

Thumbprint with red colour.

Hello Colour Yellow

Touch the pictures. Name what you see.

yellow smilie

mango

yellow crayon

banana

sunflower

chick

Trace and colour.

Hello Colour Blue

Touch the pictures. Name what you see.

water

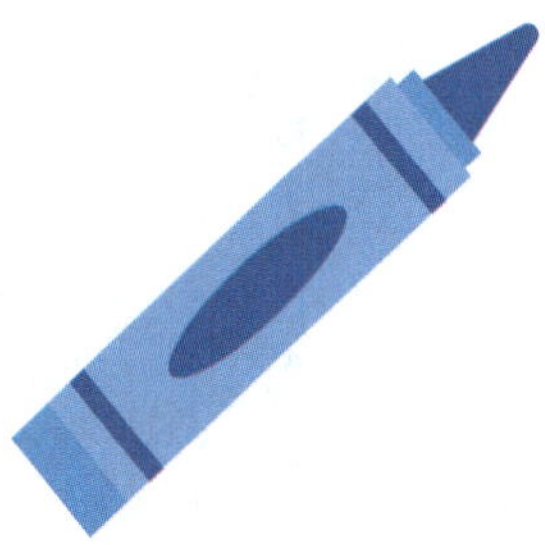

blue crayon

blue whale

ink

sky

Colour 4 beads , 3 beads and 2 beads .

I Know!

Print 3 leaves with yellow, blue and red.

Match the objects of the same colour.

Colour as shown.

Colour and complete the pattern.

Food I Like to Eat

Tick (✓) the food items you like to eat.

Baby Owl Eats Healthy

Sing.

Three baby owls fly by night and day
One day, one baby owl in the nest did stay
Mamma owl asked the little one
'Why did you not fly to have fun?'
'My tummy hurts,' said the little one.
'I will not fly and have fun.'
'Oh! You naughty one. Have fruits,
Have vegetables if you want to be fine.
Your pain will go away in no time.'
Now three baby owls fly on and on
And there is none in the nest left alone.

Zuzu and Bella

Look at the pictures. Talk about them.

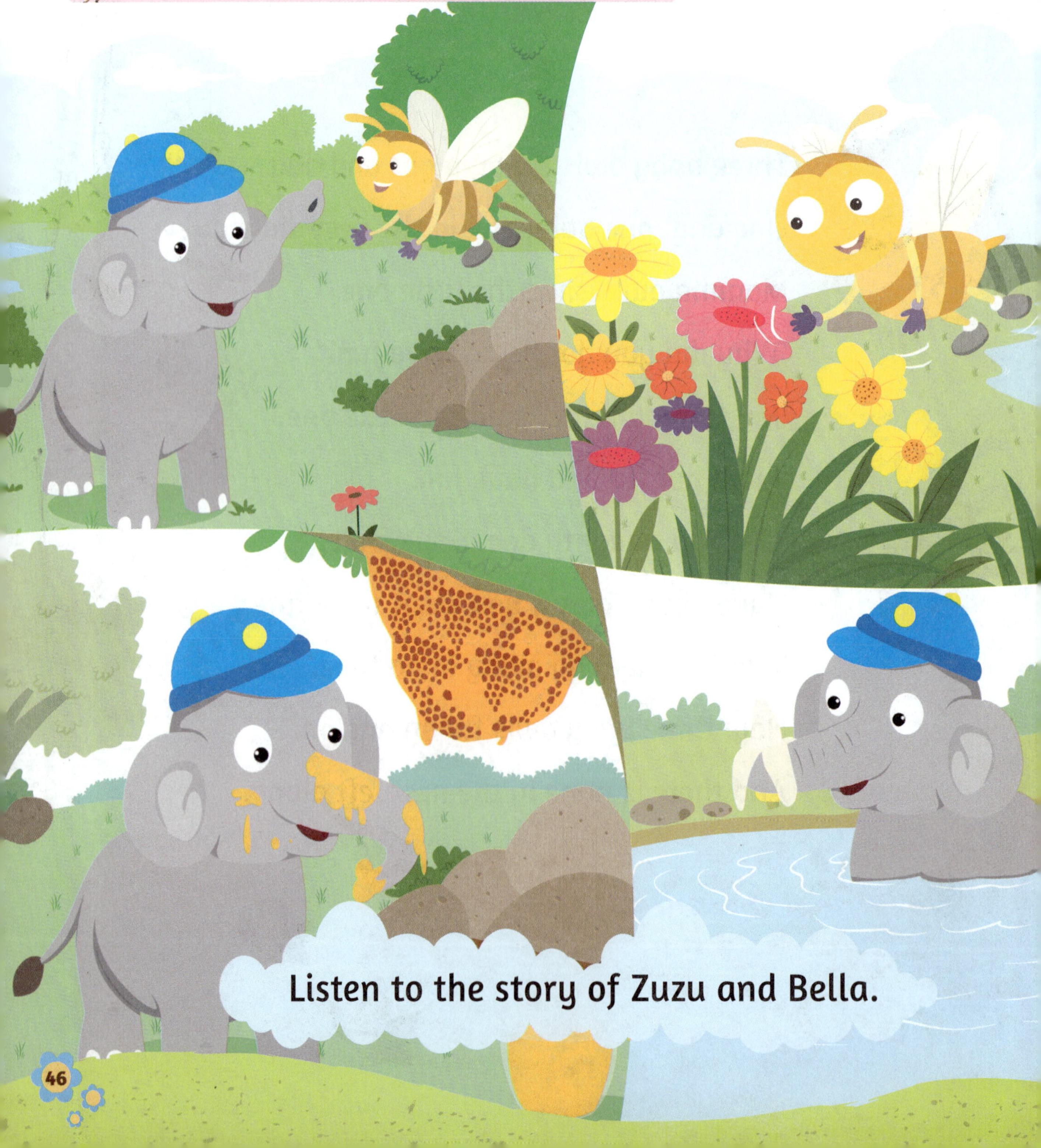

Listen to the story of Zuzu and Bella.

swing
yoga
dustbin
bush
flower

I Know!

Cross (X) the odd one out.

Look at these pictures. Which one do you like the most? Talk about it.

Cross (✗) the things not found in a park.

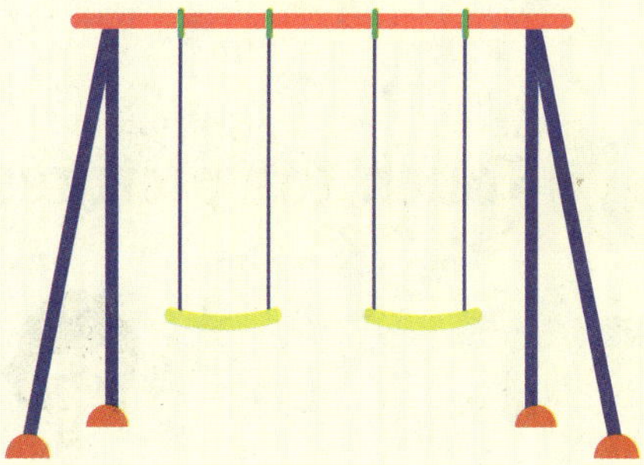

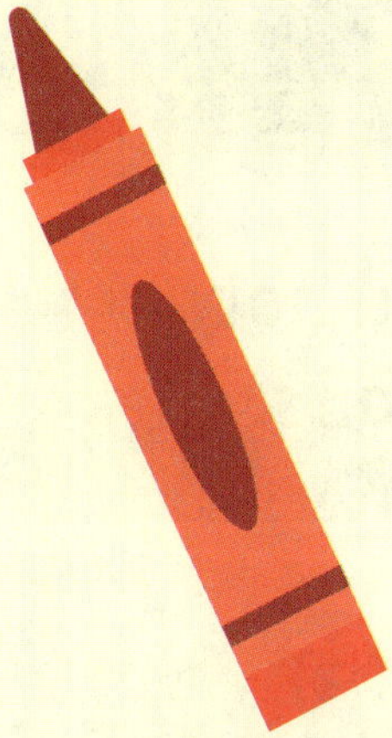

Keeping Safe

Touch the pictures. Talk about them.

We should always walk with an elder.

We should not run on stairs.

We should not talk to a stranger.

We should not scribble on walls.

Ali and Sally

Look at the pictures. Talk about them.

Listen to a story about Ali and Sally snail.

Hello Black and White

Touch the pictures. Talk about them.

chess board

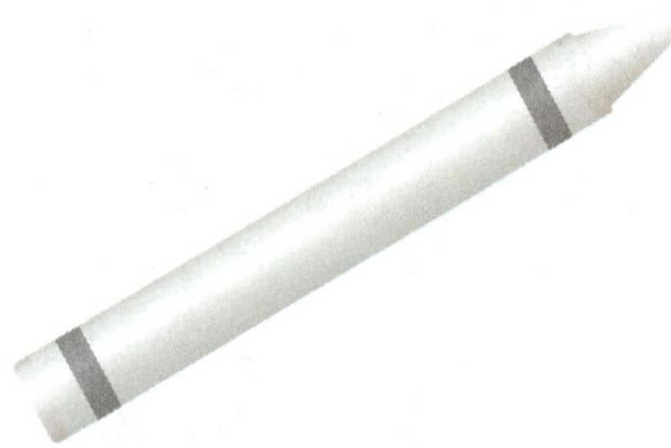

white crayon

black crayon

football

zebra

Paste cotton to make snowflakes.

Use black paint to fill all the circles.

Days of the Week

Sing.

Seven brothers come on seven days, Sunday, Monday, Tuesday, Wednesday, Thursday, Friday and Saturday.

'Hello! We make up a week,' they say.

Hello! I am **Sunday**,
I am the day to rest and pray.

Hello! I am **Monday**,
I am the day to start work and play.

Hello! I am **Tuesday**,
I come after Monday.

Hello! I am **Wednesday**,
I come in the middle of the week.

Hello! I am **Thursday**,
I say that the end is not far away.

Hello! I am **Friday**,
I say the week has gone away.

Hello! I am **Saturday**,
I say rest, for a new week is on its way.

Seven brothers come on seven days,

Sunday, Monday, Tuesday, Wednesday, Thursday, Friday and Saturday.

'Hello! We make up a week,' they say.

Paste correct stickers.

SUNDAY

MONDAY

TUESDAY

WEDNESDAY

THURSDAY

FRIDAY

SATURDAY

WEEK

I Know!

Tear and paste newspaper to make the shell of the snail.

Sing.

I am a panda, my name is Piku.
See my colour, it is black and white too.
I like to eat shoots of bamboo.

Paste correct stickers.

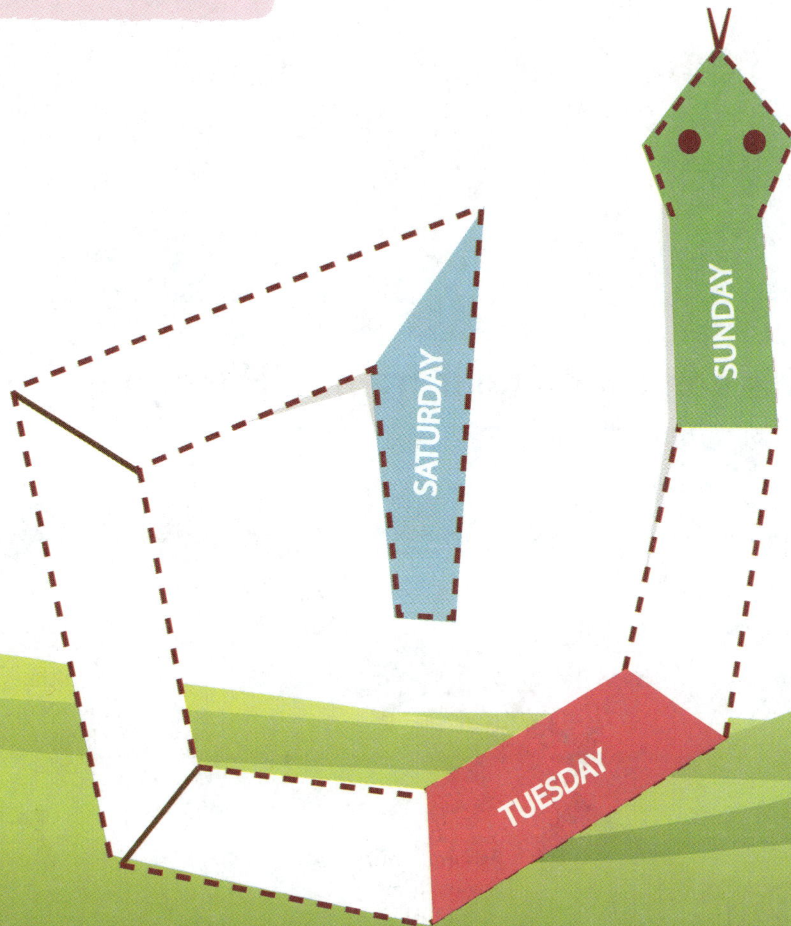

Tick (✓) the images that show the right thing.

Game

Play this game with your friends. Have fun!

SUNDAY

MONDAY

TUESDAY

WEDNESDAY

THURSDAY

FRIDAY

SATURDAY

MONDAY

WEDNESDAY

THURSDAY

FRIDAY

Sticker Page